52

QUESTIONS

FOR FRIENDS

**LEARN MORE ABOUT YOUR FRIENDS
ONE QUESTION AT A TIME**

Improve your life. Change your world.

Hatherleigh Press is committed to preserving
and protecting the natural resources of the earth.
Environmentally responsible and sustainable practices
are embraced within the company's
mission statement.
Visit us at www.hatherleighpress.com and register online
for free offers, discounts, special events,
and more.

52 Questions for a Better Friendship
Text copyright © 2017 Travis Hellstrom

Library of Congress Cataloging-in-Publication Data is available upon request.
ISBN: 978-1-57826-689-0

Printed in the United States
10 9 8 7 6 5 4 3 2 1

DEDICATION

This book is dedicated to my best friends, Jonathan and Michael, who always know the right questions to ask; and to all those wonderful friends out there who give us the space to let us truly be ourselves.

CONTENTS

Introduction
1

52 Questions
5

Resources
113

Make the Questions a Game
115

Inspirations
117

About the Author
119

INTRODUCTION

This simple book is designed to help you build a stronger friendship with someone you care for.

These questions are meant to help you start a great conversation, reconnect with who you really are, learn more about yourself and your friends, and build deeper friendships with the people who are important to you. They are also meant to complement my other book, *52 Questions for a Better Relationship*.

You will find that some questions are categorized as "Light", some are "Fun", and some are "Deep". I've used these categories so you can easily flip through the book and see the type of question on the top of the page. No matter which kind of question you encounter, I hope all of them are fun for you. I also left blank space to the left of each question for you to add notes and thoughts from your conversations.

I hope you enjoy this book, whether you are asking one question a week (which will conveniently take you exactly one year) or just jumping in and asking them whenever you like.

Good luck and have fun!

Travis

Can I ask you a
question?

Socrates

52 QUESTIONS

light

What have I said
that has helped you
the most?

What does your ideal day look like?

fun

What movie can you recite every line of?

What advice would you give to yourself five years ago?

light

If you could own a business and money wasn't an issue, what type of business would it be?

light

What's your favorite color?

If you could only work 20 hours each week, how would you spend your free time?

fun

If you had a band, what kind of band would it be and what would you name it?

What do you think I am afraid of?

fun

What would your dream house look like?

deep

What do you think is
holding me back?

deep

What could I improve on?

light

What's one of your most embarrassing moments?

What are you most
proud of?

What do you want to be remembered for?

What do I do that annoys you?

What do you do
that you think
annoys me?

What are three of
my best qualities?

What is one thing I could work on that would have the most impact on my life?

When have I disappointed you?

What do you think
I could be doing to
be happier?

fun

What is one thing
you are passionate
about right now?

What are some
qualities of people
around me that are
hurting me?

What's something you think I'd love learning in the next year?

deep

What have I said
that has hurt you
the most?

Where do you see me in five years?

What are you most proud of that you've accomplished in the last year?

deep

28

What's your mission
statement for
your life?

What's your fondest
memory of us?

fun

Do you remember
when you first
saw me?

fun

What was your first
impression of me?

What are five things you do to relax?

light

What do you think I would be really good at teaching?

What's a way you think I could make $1,000 in the next month?

What is the best
pizza you have ever
had?

deep

What do you think I could be doing to be more healthy?

fun

Who would play
me if a movie were
made about my life?

What is something I did in the past that really surprised you?

What are three ways
I've changed since
we've known each
other?

What's one thing I've done to help you in a difficult situation?

If you were guaranteed to succeed, what's the number one thing you would do?

light

What are three reasons we're still friends?

deep

What do people
think of me?

deep

What's one thing you know about me that no one else knows?

deep

What's the number
one thing I can learn
to improve my life?

light

Do you think I could
survive in the
Peace Corps?

What do you think I could be doing to be more successful?

What's one artistic skill you wish you could develop?

If you could hang out with anyone in history for a day, who would it be?

What did you want
to be when you
grew up?

fun

Where would you
choose to travel
if money was
no object?

light

What are the most
important qualities
you look for in
friends?

Judge a man by his questions rather than his answers.

Voltaire

RESOURCES

MAKE THE QUESTIONS A GAME

Over the years, I have had the pleasure of testing these questions out on lots of my family and friends. In this section you'll find some suggestions and examples on how to use the questions in this book.

FOLLOW THE LEADER

Choose a group leader or "game host" to help lead the discussion and remember, there are no right or wrong answers and no time limit.

HOT POTATO

Pass the book to a new "answerer". The answerer flips to a random question in the book and reads it aloud to the group. Then the answerer shares their response. If they have difficulty with the question, anyone else is welcome to contribute. After the first question is discussed, pass the book and move on to the next person who is now the new answerer.

ONE TO ONE

A new reader holds the book and picks a question or flips to a random page in the book. The reader chooses someone who they would like to have answer the question and reads the question to them. They share their answer with the group.

CHANGELING

A new reader holds the book and picks a question or flips to a random page in the book. The reader reads or alters a question. Each question is simply a starting point. The reader can take it in any direction they desire. The most important thing is to have fun!

INSPIRATIONS

I have many wonderful people, resources, and inspirations to thank for this book. Here are a few I highly recommend you check out. You can also visit www.travishellstrom. com/52 to download an interactive PDF with links to these books, talks, and much more.

- *A More Beautiful Question* by Warren Berger
- *How Will You Measure Your Life* by Clayton Christensen
- *Pivot* by Jenny Blake
- *Coaching Questions* by Tony Stoltzfus
- *Essentialism* by Greg McKeown
- *The Coaching Habit* by Michael Bungay Stanier

ABOUT THE AUTHOR

Travis Hellstrom is an optimist, husband, professor and author who helps people dream big and expand their influence. He is a Returned Peace Corps Volunteer and Founder of Advance Humanity. He is the author of *The Peace Corps Volunteer's Handbook* and *The Dalai Lama Book of Quotes*. To read more from Travis, visit www.travishellstrom.com.